Thirds in Thumb Position
for the Cello

Book Two

by Cassia Harvey

CHP212

©2011 by C. Harvey Publications All Rights Reserved.

www.charveypublications.com - print books
www.learnstrings.com - PDF downloadable books
www.harveystringarrangements.com - chamber music

Thirds in Thumb Position for the Cello
1

Book Two

Cassia Harvey

©2011 C. Harvey Publications All Rights Reserved.

2

Thirds in Thumb Position for the Cello, Book Two

3

©2011 C. Harvey Publications All Rights Reserved.

4

Thirds in Thumb Position for the Cello, Book Two

5

©2011 C. Harvey Publications All Rights Reserved.

6

Thirds in Thumb Position for the Cello, Book Two

7

8

9

10

11

12

Thirds in Thumb Position for the Cello, Book Two

13

©2011 C. Harvey Publications All Rights Reserved.

14

15

16

17

18

Thirds in Thumb Position for the Cello, Book Two

19

©2011 C. Harvey Publications All Rights Reserved.

20

21

22

23

24

25

26

27

28

Thirds in Thumb Position for the Cello, Book Two

29

30

31

32

Thirds in Thumb Position for the Cello, Book Two

33

©2011 C. Harvey Publications All Rights Reserved.

34

35

36

37

38

Thirds in Thumb Position for the Cello, Book Two

39

40

Thirds in Thumb Position for the Cello, Book Two

41

42

43

44

45

46

Available from www.charveypublications.com
Dancing Into Bethlehem: Compatible Christmas Duets for Strings

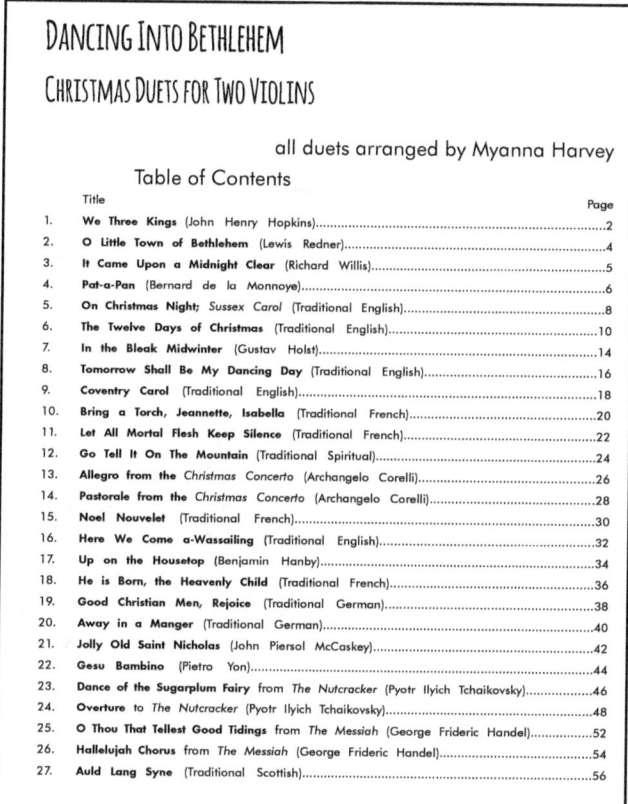

CHP360

CHP361

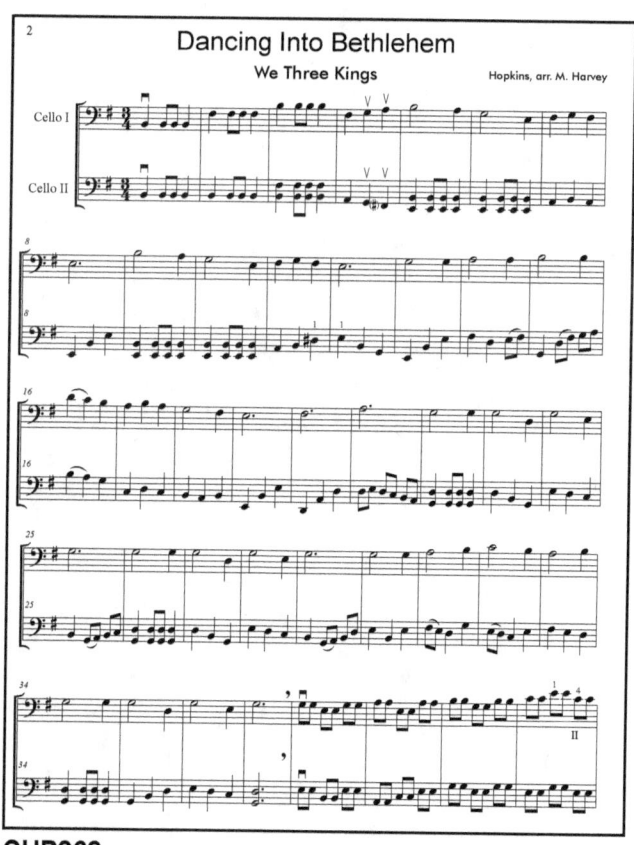

CHP362

www.ingramcontent.com/pod-product-compliance
Lightning Source LLC
Chambersburg PA
CBHW051425070526
44584CB00023B/3592